The World's Best Russian Jokes

Algis Ruksenas

The World's Best Russian Jokes

Illustrated by Louis Silvestro

ANGUS
& ROBERTSON
PUBLISHERS

ANGUS & ROBERTSON PUBLISHERS

Unit 4, Eden Park, 31 Waterloo Road,
North Ryde, NSW, Australia 2113, and
16 Golden Square, London W1R 4BN,
United Kingdom

First published in the USA, as
Is That You Laughing, Comrade?,
by Citadel Press in 1986
This revised edition first published
in Australia by Angus & Robertson
Publishers and in the United Kingdom
by Angus & Robertson (UK) in 1987

Published by arrangement with Citadel Press,
a division of Lyle Stuart, Inc.

Text copyright © 1986 by Algis Ruksenas
Illustrations copyright © 1987 by Louis Silvestro

National Library of Australia
Cataloguing-in-publication data.

Ruksenas, Algis, 1945–
    The world's best Russian jokes.

    Rev.ed.
    ISBN 0 207 15477 5.

    1. American wit and humor. I. Ruksenas, Algis
    1945–   . Is that you laughing, comrade?
    II. Silvestro, Louis, 1953–   . III. Title.
818'.5402

Typeset in 12 pt Goudy Old Style Bold
by Setrite Typesetters
Printed in the United Kingdom

I once knew an old man in Moscow who had met Stalin at the height of the Great Purge.

"I was a small boy at the time," began the old man, a look of warming nostalgia in his eyes. "My father was a kitchen hand in the Kremlin. One day, the ball I was kicking went through an open door. I rushed in after it. It was Comrade Stalin's room!"

"What happened?" I asked. "You must have been frightened."

"Oh no, you know how it is with a child sometimes. I actually asked him, 'What are you doing, comrade?' And you know," said the old man, eyes beaming, "instead of slashing my face with his razor, Stalin simply replied, 'I am shaving.' Just like that. Amazing! Yes, I'll never forget the kindness and generosity he showed me that day."

An intellectual in Moscow owned a parrot which he taught a variety of subjects. One day the parrot flew out an open window and disappeared.

The intellectual searched frantically around the city and finally hurried to KGB headquarters.

"Why do you tell us that your parrot escaped?" an official asked. "We don't have it."

"I know, comrade Commissar," the intellectual said. "But I'm sure it will turn up eventually and I just want to assure you that I don't share its political opinions."

A wayward American businessman was feeling lonely one evening during his stay in Leningrad and visited the hotel bar. He noticed a ravishing young blonde who invited his attention.

Soon they were in his room enjoying all sorts of delights of the flesh. After several engaging hours, the young woman prepared to leave.

"You haven't said anything about payment," the man inquired. "Surely you expect some payment for providing me with such an enjoyable evening and such sweet conversation."

"Oh, no. Think nothing of it," the young woman replied.

"Please, you must expect something. Perhaps you're just shy?"

"No, no," the young woman demurred.

"Please. I insist."

"Very well," she said. "Remove the intermediate range Pershing ballistic missiles from Europe!"

A Muscovite was visiting Georgia: "How is it now with meat in Georgia?"

The Georgian replied: "With meat everything is fine; *without* meat everything is awful."

Stalin dies and goes to hell.

Some time later, St Peter is surprised to see a dozen devils clamouring on the Pearly Gates to be let in.

"What do you want?" asks St Peter, suspecting some devious trick.

"We want to get in," a devil replies.

"Why?"

The devils prostrate themselves before the great saint. "We want political asylum!"

It is May Day in Moscow. Along with the members of the Central Committee on the reviewing platform are Alexander the Great, Julius Caesar and Napoleon.

Alexander the Great is obviously impressed with the enormous military parade taking place below them. "With an army like this I would have conquered the world!"

Caesar is speechless with awe. Napoleon, reading a copy of *Pravda*, does not reply.

Dozens of Mig jets scream overhead and swoop down low over the reviewing platform. Caesar exclaims: "If I had machines like those I'd bring the entire world to its knees!"

Irritated by Napoleon's absorption in *Pravda*, Alexander finally asks him, "Why don't you watch the parade? This is truly a magnificent army."

"Maybe so," replies Napoleon, "but this newspaper is amazing as well. If I'd had it, the world would never have known about Waterloo."

Comrade Vladimir Ilich Pistov left Moscow on his first trip to the West. Thoughtfully, he sent postcards to his family:

> Best wishes from free Romania. Pistov.
> Best wishes from free Czechoslovakia. Pistov.
> Best wishes from free Hungary. Pistov.
> The final one: Best wishes from Austria.
> Free Pistov.

A Soviet pessimist and a Soviet optimist.

The pessimist says: "Russia has become such hell. Everything is so bad it couldn't become worse."

The optimist says: "It will, it surely will."

During his famous visit to the United States Nikita Khrushchev became fascinated with the idea of the striptease and decided to experiment with such shows in Moscow.

Upon his return he ordered several trusted associates to open a night club where striptease would be featured and where he could gain extra funds for the Party treasury.

"Now, remember, you must do this very discreetly and only with the most trusted personnel," Khrushchev cautioned. "You know how our people are about these seemingly decadent displays."

The night club opened and the first night the aides could not control the enormous crowds; people lined up in droves to get even the slightest glimpse of the striptease.

On the second night the club was empty with not a patron in sight.

Khrushchev was puzzled and perturbed and called his aides in for an explanation.

"What happened?" he asked. "I told you to use only the most trusted personnel. You probably left this project in the hands of unreliables."

"Oh, no, Comrade Secretary," one of them replied. "We did exactly as you ordered. We used only the most trusted personnel. Galina was a Party member since 1915, Ludmila was a Party member since 1917, Natasha was a Party member since 1918, Olga . . ."

Puzzled why people persisted in believing in God under the Soviet system, Premier Mikhail Gorbachev went incognito into an authorised church to observe the worshippers.

He saw a woman approach the altar and kneel in front of a crucifix. "Tell me," she whispered devoutly, "will I see my little Vladie become an engineer and have a successful career?"

Suddenly a deep voice bellowed from the heavens. "Yes, my dear woman. Because you have been so faithful, you will see in your own lifetime the great career achievements of your son."

Soon a man knelt at the altar. He looked devoutly at the crucifix. "Tell me," he whispered, "will I see my little Ludmilla be permitted to go to medical school and become a doctor?"

"Yes," replied the imposing voice. "Because you have been so faithful in adversity, you will see in your own lifetime your loving daughter become a renowned physician."

Gorbachev was truly amazed. He crept slowly to the altar with awe and trepidation and murmured devoutly as he looked at the crucifix: "Tell me, will I see the banner of communism spread throughout the entire world?"

Boomed the heavenly voice: "Not in *my* lifetime!"

Three doctors at an international conference were discussing the frustrations involved in their calling.

"We try hard to save people," a French specialist said. "But you know how modern medicine is; we treat them for diabetes and they end up dying of heart disease."

"I know what you mean," agreed an American colleague. "We treat them for high blood pressure and they end up dying of old age."

"We have no such frustrations," declared a Russian doctor. "When we treat them for a disease, they die of that disease."

The Sino-Soviet rivalry increased to such a level that China and Russia finally went to war.

On the first day the Soviets captured one million Chinese soldiers. On the second day the Soviets captured another million Chinese soldiers. On the third day they captured yet another million Chinese soldiers. This went on daily until by the sixth day the Soviets had six million Chinese soldiers on their hands.

On the seventh day the Chinese commander sent a message to the Soviet commander: "Do you surrender?"

During the height of détente Brezhnev was dallying one night with a young woman in the Kremlin.

Outside, people were clamouring to be permitted to emigrate to the West.

"Leonid, my sweet," the young woman said, "why don't you give those poor people their wish?"

"Ahhh, you little fox," Brezhnev replied with an expectant smile. "You want it to be just me and you."

Question: What would happen if you built communism in the Sahara?

Answer: Everything would be fine for the first three years, but then there would be an acute shortage of sand.

Roman Grynberg, that famous man of letters, advisor to three administrations, long-time Party member and decorated hero of the Great Patriotic War, had applied for an exit visa to Israel. He was told to report to the local Party committee.

"How dare you," began his interrogator. "How dare you — such a prominent and distinguished Soviet citizen — choose to defect to that hole, Israel!"

"Comrade," replied the rather agitated Grynberg. "You may not believe this, but I am strongly against the move. My wife wants to go and you know how a woman can make your life hell."

"What? My God, man, listen to what you're saying! You have served on powerful government committees. You have given orders that have changed the face of this country — and you cannot deal with your own wife?"

"Well, my wife really isn't the worst of it," said Grynberg, pausing to lick his dry lips. "My mother-in-law is a demon. Every day it's the same: 'Let's go to Israel . . . Let's go to Israel . . .'"

"Come now, comrade," scoffed his interrogator. "During the war you were in command of a regiment. You distinguished yourself in battle. And now you're giving in to your mother-in-law. Why, it's like a bad joke!"

Grynberg, a pathetic figure by now, was at his wits' end. "Look, I suppose I could handle my wife and her mother if it wasn't for my children. Every day they embarrass me in public with their pleas to go to Israel. They just will not stay here."

"Listen to me, Grynberg. You have been a faithful

Party member for forty years, and now you can't even explain things to your own children?"

Grynberg had had enough. Throwing his hands up in the air, he exploded: "What do you want from me? What am I supposed to do when I'm the only Jew in the whole damn family?!"

Question: What is the difference between socialism and capitalism?

Answer: Capitalism is based on the exploitation of one human being by another human being, but socialism is just the opposite.

A Moscow housewife went shopping for goods. She went to one store for bread and found a line stretching around the block, so she went to another store for milk. The line there was just as long. Growing more frustrated, she thought she would try the GUM department store for toilet paper. The lines were twice as long as the others.

Totally frustrated, she went to buy some vodka, but found the wait there just as long.

Returning home empty-handed she told her husband the same old story about unending lines.

"I'll take care of this once and for all," her husband replied in a rage as he pulled a revolver from a hiding place behind the wall. "I'm personally going to the Kremlin to shoot the Premier."

When he got there he found a line of five hundred people waiting ahead of him.

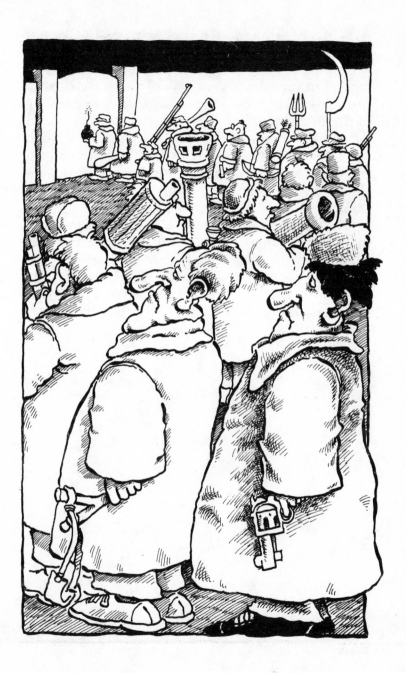

An Englishman, a Frenchman, and a Russian were discussing happiness.

"Happiness for me," said the Englishman, "is to pick a beautiful autumn weekend and go to my country estate where I invite my friends to go riding to the hounds."

"Ahhh. Happiness for me," said the Frenchman, "is to meet my sweetheart in May on the banks of the Seine where we picnic with wine, bread and cheese in the shadow of the magnificent Notre Dame."

"And happiness for me," said the Russian, "is to sit in my one-room flat in Moscow with my little Vladie on my knee, reading to him the editorial from *Pravda*. And when the secret police come to the door and ask: 'Is your name Ivan Ivanovich?' happiness for me is to say: 'No. He lives upstairs.'"

A Lithuanian worker was walking along a Baltic beach when he noticed an ancient lamp sticking out of the sand. He picked it up and with idle curiosity began rubbing the sides, whereupon a genie appeared and offered him three wishes.

Amazed at this magical occurrence the worker blurted out: "I want China to invade Lithuania."

The genie agreed to the first wish and asked what else he wished for.

"I want China to invade Lithuania again," the worker repeated.

The genie was a little puzzled, wondering why the worker would ask twice for such a strange wish. "You have only one wish left," the genie reminded. "Think carefully about your life's greatest desire and I will grant it."

"I want China to invade Lithuania," the worker declared once more.

"Why in the world would you want China to invade Lithuania three times?" the genie asked with intense curiosity.

"Because it would have to cross Russia six times."

During his heyday Brezhnev was embarrassed on more than one occasion by broadcasts over the BBC which transmitted information that could only have come from the inner circles of the Soviet government.

He became so perturbed that one day he locked up the entire Politburo in one of the meeting halls of the Kremlin and declared: "No-one will leave this room until the guilty one confesses that he has been leaking information to the BBC."

One hour went by. Another. Still another.

Soon Chernenko approached Brezhnev and told him he had to go to the bathroom.

"No!" Brezhnev declared. "No-one leaves the room until the guilty one confesses he has been leaking information to the BBC."

Soon there was a knock on the door. Brezhnev opened it to see a charwoman holding a roll of toilet paper.

"What do you want?" he asked in a huff.

"I just heard on the BBC that Chernenko has diarrhoea."

An Armenian black marketeer was flying to Moscow with two crates of fresh oranges. En route the plane was hijacked to France where the entire contingent of passengers, except the Armenian, asked for political asylum.

The plane returned to Moscow with the Armenian who was greeted by officials as a state hero.

Later a friend asked why he did not defect when he had the chance.

"Idiot!" he declared. "Do you think I could have sold all these oranges in Paris?"

Joseph Stalin wanted to get a true picture of what people thought of him so he went incognito into a movie theatre.

After the feature a newsreel came on which naturally highlighted him in every scene. All the people in the theatre stood up amid thunderous, unrelenting applause. Stalin modestly remained seated.

After a few moments the man next to him nudged Stalin and said: "Most people feel the same way you do, comrade. But it would be safer if you stood up."

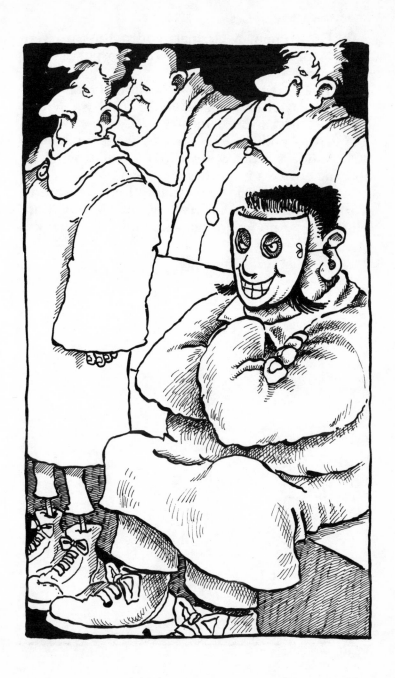

A Frenchman, a German and a Russian were boasting about the modes of transportation at their disposal.

"I drive a Renault to work," said the Frenchman. "On Sundays I drive my Peugeot. And when I go abroad, I drive a Citroën."

"I drive a Volkswagen to work," said the German. "On Sundays I drive my BMW. And when I go abroad, I drive a Mercedes."

"As for me," said the Russian, "I take the bus to work. On Sundays I drive around in my little Moskvitch. And when I go abroad, I drive a tank."

A Polish worker went to a local bank to deposit his wages. Worried about the dire conditions of the Polish economy, he inquired what would happen if the bank collapsed.

"All our deposits are guaranteed by the Ministry of Finance," the teller replied.

"But what if the Ministry of Finance could not honour the guarantee?" the worker persisted.

"In that case the Polish government itself would intercede," the teller said with growing irritation.

"But what if the government would go bankrupt?" the worker asked with undiminished concern.

"In that case our socialist comrades in the Soviet Union would naturally come to our assistance," the teller retorted.

"But what if the Soviet Union collapsed?" the Polish worker persisted.

"Idiot!" snapped the teller. "Isn't that worth losing one week's wages?"

Question: Why do the secret police always travel in threes?

Answer: One can read, another can write, and the third keeps an eye on the two intellectuals.

A commissar overheard a worker muttering foreign words to himself.

"What in the world are you mumbling?" the commissar inquired.

"I'm learning Hebrew."

"Hebrew? Why are you wasting your time on Hebrew?"

"For when I go to heaven," the worker explained.

"What makes you so sure you're going to heaven?" the commissar smirked. "How do you know you're not going to hell?"

"In that case, I already know Russian."

A teacher in a provincial school asked a pupil to use the word "communists" in a sentence.

"My cat just had kittens and they are all good communists," recited Ivan.

"Very good, my little comrade," said the teacher. Several weeks later the teacher asked the same pupil to use the word "capitalists" in a sentence.

"My cat had kittens recently and they are all good capitalists," Ivan recited.

The teacher was taken aback. "You told me the kittens were all good communists. How can they be good capitalists now?"

"Comrade Teacher, they've opened their eyes now."

A commissar was visiting a collective farm to check on the season's crops.

"How are the potatoes?" he inquired.

"The potatoes are so plentiful," a farmer replied, "that if we put them end to end they will touch the feet of God."

"How can that be?" blurted the commissar. "There is no God."

"Well, there are no potatoes either."

In Leningrad there is a rumour that the schools will soon teach three foreign languages. English and Hebrew for those who plan to leave, and Chinese for those who plan to stay.

A Russian, an American, a Frenchman and a Lithuanian were among passengers in an airliner. Suddenly the pilot appeared and said the plane was losing altitude due to a mechanical failure.

"Three of you will have to sacrifice yourselves if we are to save the others," the pilot said reluctantly.

Whereupon the American shouted, "Long live free America!" and jumped out the hatch.

Not to be outdone, the Frenchman yelled, "Long live free France!" and followed the American out the hatch.

"Long live free Lithuania!" shouted the Lithuanian as he grabbed the Russian and threw him out the hatch after them.

During his last years Brezhnev was rushed to a Moscow hospital for emergency surgery.

"Is this it? Is he dying?" a frantic doctor asked.

"No," another replied. "We just have to widen his ribcage. There's no more room on his chest for his medals."

A citizen is being interrogated by the KGB.

"Which of my eyes is artificial?" toys the interrogator. "If you guess, I'll let you go."

"The left one," replies the citizen without hesitation.

"How did you know?" asks the official with genuine surprise.

"It has a more kindly look about it."

After he died, Stalin was given the choice of whether he wanted to go to heaven or hell. He asked to see what each was like and St Peter took him on a tour.

In heaven Stalin saw a quiet, placid scene with people walking around meadows and enjoying a serene spiritual existence.

In hell he saw a noisy hall with a wall-to-wall bar around which sat jovial people talking, laughing and drinking. A 20-piece orchestra played lively music while gorgeous young women danced and cavorted.

"Aha. This is for me," Stalin declared and asked to be let into hell.

As soon as St Peter handed him over to Lucifer, the devil grabbed Stalin by the scruff of the neck and took him to a chamber filled with pots of boiling oil.

As he was being tossed into one of the pots, Stalin protested: "But . . . but what about the dance hall? What about the music? What about the dancing girls?"

"That," replied the devil, "was just propaganda."

An Englishman, a Frenchman, and a Russian were arguing about the nationality of Adam and Eve.

"They must have been English," the Englishman offered. "After all, only a gentleman would share his last apple with a lady."

"They surely were French," the Frenchman asserted. "They were so hopelessly in love."

"They could only have been Russian," declared the Russian. "Who else would walk around naked, have nothing but an apple to eat between them, and think they were in paradise?"

Some time before his death, President Brezhnev was addressing a Party gathering. As always, he began reading from notes extracted from his suit pocket.

"Comrades!" Brezhnev intoned. "We are all saddened today at the death of our beloved leader . . . General Secretary of the Central Committee — " He paused in bewilderment: "President . . . of . . . the . . . Presidium . . . of the . . . Supreme . . . Soviet —" A much longer pause: "Leonid . . . Ilyich . . . Brezh . . . Excuse me, comrades," Brezhnev explained. "I think I've put on Comrade Andropov's jacket by mistake."

As Stalin was being removed from the mausoleum in Red Square, Lenin turned to him with a quizzical look.

"The housing shortage has eased up," Stalin said. "I've found a place of my own."

Question: What is the Moscow String Quartet?

Answer: The Moscow Symphony Orchestra just back from a Western tour.

A Party screening committee was interviewing candidates for the secret police.

They asked the first candidate: "What is two plus two?"

"Three," replied the candidate.

"Try again," urged a member of the committee.

"Seven."

"One more time."

"Six."

The committee dismissed the candidate and wrote on his application: "Ignorant, but imaginative. Accepted."

They asked the second candidate: "What is two plus two?"

"Three."

"Try again," urged another committee member.

"Three," repeated the candidate.

"One more time."

"Three," the candidate persisted.

The committee dismissed the candidate and wrote on his application: "Ignorant, but determined. Accepted."

A third candidate came in.

"What is two plus two?"

"Four," the candidate said.

The committee immediately dismissed him and wrote on his application: "Educated. Keep under surveillance."

A citizen shopping for food walks into a store with empty shelves.

"Hmmm. I see you have no bread," the disappointed shopper comments.

"You're wrong, comrade. We sell fish here. We have no fish," corrects the clerk. "The store that has no bread is down the block."

Although Nikita Khrushchev was not permitted to go to Disneyland during his trip to the United States due to security considerations, President Eisenhower did offer to take him for a ride on a vintage train.

As they were chugging along a winding road, there appeared from nowhere a band of whooping Indians who gave lively chase on their horses.

The President suddenly felt embarrassed and threatened.

"Quick!" he ordered as the Indians gained ground on the train, "get me a million dollars in small bills!" He received the money and tossed it out a window, hoping the Indians would halt their attack.

The Indians ignored the bills fluttering around them and steadily gained ground.

Observing all this, Khrushchev asked for a pencil and paper. He scribbled something on it and tossed it out the window. The chief caught it, read it, and within seconds all the Indians stopped in their tracks, turned tail, and galloped at full speed away from the train.

"How did you do that?" asked the President with astonishment and relief. "What did you write?"

"Oh, it was nothing," declared Khrushchev. "I simply wrote: 'This road leads to communism.'"

A citizen came upon a friend hurrying to the subway and lugging two heavy suitcases.

"Hello Ivan! How are you? I haven't seen you since you returned from your visit to the West."

"I know," Ivan replied. "I've been busy."

"What did you bring home?"

"Oh, many things," Ivan replied, putting down the heavy suitcases. "Look at this fancy wristwatch." He showed a modern timepiece to his friend and proudly demonstrated its features. "Do you want to know what time it is in New York?"

"Of course. What time is it?"

Ivan pushed a button and the time in New York appeared on the display.

"That's amazing!" his friend exclaimed. "And it's so small! Now, what about the time in Bombay?"

Ivan pushed another button and Bombay time appeared on the display screen.

"You want me to calculate for you when the next solar eclipse will be?" Ivan asked.

"Sure!" exclaimed his friend.

Ivan pushed some more buttons and the date, time and year of the next solar eclipse appeared on the display screen.

"That Western technology is amazing!" the friend exclaimed. "But how are you going to replace the batteries? You know we don't have special batteries for such precision equipment here."

"That's all right," Ivan said, proudly looking at his timepiece. "I adapted my own batteries."

"Oh? How did you do that?"

"You're looking at them," Ivan said, as he pointed to the two suitcases.

A Soviet citizen who was visiting the West was besieged by many questions from persons wanting to know more about communism.

"You mean to tell me," asked a curious host, "that by being a communist you share everything?"

"Yes," came the reply.

"You mean, if you had two houses, you would give me one?"

"Of course."

"And if you had two cars, you would give me one?"

"Certainly."

"And if you had two stoves, or televisions or refrigerators, you would give me one of each?"

"Naturally."

"And if you had two shirts, you would give me one?"

"No!" replied the communist emphatically.

"Why not?"

"Because I *have* two shirts."

An American reporter at the Geneva summit meeting was asking a Russian official about the Soviet constitution.

"Our constitution is an outstanding document," the Soviet official boasted. "It's just like yours. It guarantees freedom of expression."

Asked the reporter: "But does it guarantee freedom after expression?"

Two old friends meet on a street in Volgograd.

"How's life treating you?" asks one.

"Just great," replies the other.

"Have you been reading the papers?"

"Of course. How else would I know?"

Social scientists wanting to test the ingenuity of the British, French, Spanish, Russians, and Lithuanians, placed two men and a woman of each nationality onto a remote island with nothing but lumber at their disposal.

Some months later the scientists returned to see what happened.

They came upon the British and saw three neat cottages with fences surrounding small gardens.

"How are you doing?" the scientists asked the man at the first cottage.

"Jolly good," he replied.

"How are your neighbours?"

"I don't know. We haven't been properly introduced," replied the Englishman.

The scientists came upon the French and saw two cottages.

"How are you doing?" they asked at the first cottage.

"*Bon, bon,*" replied a man who was seated with a woman on a small couch.

"And how about madame?"

"Oh, she is just fine," the man replied. "One week she is my wife and my neighbour's lover, and the next week she is my neighbour's wife and my lover."

The scientists jotted down some notes and continued on their way. Soon they saw the Spanish area where a woman dressed in black was kneeling at a gravesite mourning over two wooden crosses.

The scientists continued on their way and came upon the Russians. Two men were sitting around a makeshift table, playing cards. Their lumber was missing.

"How is everything?" the scientists asked.

"Normal," the Russians replied.

"Where is your woman?"

"The proletariat? Oh, she's out in the fields working," they said as they continued playing.

The scientists continued on until they came upon the Lithuanians. They found all three standing around expectantly. Nearby were stakes marking areas where cottages were to be built. Their lumber was neatly stacked in three piles.

"Why haven't you started building?" asked the scientists.

"Well ..." replied one of the Lithuanians. "Maybe the government will change ..."

Once upon a time there was a man walking along a deserted country road in the middle of winter. It was very icy and the snow was beginning to thicken, and the man, wearing only a thin coat, was shivering violently.

Engrossed as he was in the task of getting home, he just happened to spy a little bird lying on the road, seemingly frozen solid. The man's heart went out to it. "We are birds of a feather," he thought, as he picked the bird up and put it down his trousers in the hope that his own body heat would revive it. Half an hour later, the man felt a flutter between his legs and was very happy that the bird was still alive. But he knew that what was needed was real heat, something the man just could not provide.

Right at that moment a cow in a nearby pasture voided itself of a big, steaming load. Realising that this could provide the warmth the bird so desperately needed, the man walked over and stuck the lucky creature into the steaming pile. He walked away, happy that he had saved its life.

And sure enough, very soon the bird *was* revived. Happy to be alive, it started whistling notes of pure joy. But a fox happened to be nearby, heard the song, followed it to its source and ate the bird.

This typical Russian peasant fable has three morals: one, it's not only your enemies that get you into it; two, it's not always your friends who get you out; and three, if you're in it up to your neck, don't open your mouth.

Two intellectuals were discussing the destiny of the Soviet Union.

"What do you think our future will be like in two or three years?"

"Don't ask me. I don't even know what our past will be like in two or three years."

During the recent troubles in Afghanistan, a Soviet officer watched in amazement as ten of his fully armed soldiers were chased by one Afghan tribesman wielding an ancient scimitar.

"You cowards!" he screamed. "Why are you running? There's only one Afghan behind you."

"That's true, sir," one of them managed to say as he rushed past. "But we don't know exactly which one of us he's chasing."

Lenin dies and arrives at the Pearly Gates. He sees St Peter and asks to be let in.

"You can't come in here," St Peter replies. "You agitated and instigated revolution! You're a troublemaker! Go to hell, where you belong!"

Lenin shrugs his shoulders and turns away.

Some time later St Peter comes to hell to check on Lucifer and see if everything is being administered according to the Providential plan.

"Sorry, I can't talk now," says Lucifer curtly as he glances at his watch. "I'm late for a Party rally."

A foreign correspondent, renowned for his objectivity and open-mindedness, wanted to gauge the people's real feelings about Stalin. He knew it would be a difficult task, because everyone was literally afraid of his own shadow under the tyrant's rule. Still, the reporter, with his innocent curiosity, would try.

"Tell me," the reporter would ask earnestly of various passers-by. "What do you *really* think of Stalin?"

A look of abject fear or a blank stare would greet him and the people would scurry away. Finally, one day he encountered a man who looked like someone who would speak up.

"Tell me, what do you *really* think of Stalin?" the reporter asked.

The man stopped short, seemed startled at first, then peered over each shoulder and muttered to the reporter: "Follow me."

They went along Lenin Prospekt, approached Red Square, crossed it hurriedly and entered a nearby building, with the man always looking behind him to see if they were being followed.

He led the reporter out the back door of the building and through the streets of Moscow, always changing direction at intersections. They entered the GUM department store, mingled with the crowd and left through another door. The man's eyes kept darting left and right as he motioned the reporter to follow along.

They hailed a taxi and travelled aimlessly through Moscow until they arrived at Gorky Park. The man looked around some more and led the reporter to a small lake in the park where he rented a rowboat, still peering suspiciously over his shoulders.

He rowed the reporter into the middle of the lake, looked around one more time, leaned over and whispered into the reporter's ear: "I like him."

Brezhnev was visiting a collective farm. He asked a young girl whether she recognised him. The girl stared at him blankly.

"Don't you know me? I'm the one who's given you everything you have," Brezhnev prodded.

"Papa! Papa!" the girl cried. "Uncle Peter is here from America!"

A man was sitting in his apartment when he heard a loud knock on the door.

"Who is it?" he asked apprehensively.

"It is the Angel of Death."

"Whew. Thank goodness. For a minute I thought it was the secret police."

An American tourist visiting Russia got into a heated exchange with a Muscovite about the relative merits of their political systems.

"We live in a free country," the tourist declared. "We can say anything we want and not be afraid of any kind of punishment."

"We live in a free country, too," the Russian countered. "We can say anything we want and not be afraid of any kind of punishment either."

"I don't believe it," the tourist said. "Why, if I wanted to, I'm free to go to the US embassy right now and shout all kinds of slogans against our president."

"So what?" the Muscovite replied. "I'm free to go to the US embassy right now and shout all kinds of slogans against your president too."

Two workers at a match factory were murmuring to each other during an awards ceremony for the Order of Lenin.

"What's going on?" one asked.

"Our factory director is being awarded the Order of Lenin."

"For what?"

"A saboteur tried to set fire to an ammunition depot with our matches."

"So why is the factory director getting the Order of Lenin?"

"The matches wouldn't light."

A Western tourist visiting Moscow wanted to see as many attractions as possible.

He went to Moscow's finest restaurant, but was told the tables were taken. The tourist pondered a moment, then said: "Well, let me order two tables, but just take one place. The rest of the places you can use at your own discretion."

Without hesitation, the tourist was seated.

After a delicious and special meal, attended to by solicitous waiters, the tourist decided to see a performance of the world-renowned Bolshoi Ballet.

"I'd like to buy a ticket to the ballet," the tourist said at the box office.

He was told all the seats were sold out.

"In that case, I'd like to buy half a dozen tickets," the tourist said. "But I need just one for myself. The rest you can use at your own discretion," he told the ticket attendant.

Within minutes the tourist had one of the best seats in the house.

After the performance, he decided to visit Lenin's Mausoleum in Red Square. He encountered a line hundreds of metres long.

"My visit is very short," the tourist explained to the guards. "Is there any way I can get in past this line?"

"Sorry," the guards replied. "You'll have to wait like everybody else."

"In that case, we should have a drink while I'm waiting," the tourist said as he produced several bottles of vodka and offered them to the guards.

The guards eagerly accepted a bottle each and

declared: "Do you want to go in and see him, or would you like us to bring him out here?"

A Frenchman, an American and a Russian came together to exchange tales about their countries.

The Frenchman began by saying: "When I buy my Catherine a new bra and she puts it on, the fabric rips. It's not because we French make poor quality lingerie, but because Catherine has such large breasts."

The American countered with: "When my Cathy sits on a pony, her feet reach the ground. It's not because American ponies are so small, but because my Cathy has such beautiful long legs."

Finally, the Russian topped them all with this: "When I'm on my way to work in the morning, I slap my Katya on the bottom. When I finish work her behind is still wobbling like jelly. But it's not that my Katya has a fat bottom, it's just that we in the Soviet Union have such a short working day."

A student had graduated with high honours from the university, but could not find work in his chosen field.

He complained to the local Party headquarters, where the secretary said he could find the student work at the local zoo.

"The lion just died there," the Party official explained. "We could dress you up as a lion until we get another one."

The student agreed and soon found himself in the lion's cage dressed as the king of beasts. He was pleased with the chance to work and even enjoyed his assignment, until, one evening, upon leaving his cage, he wandered by accident into the holding cage of a large tiger.

"What in the world am I going to do now?" the student muttered fearfully as the tiger came towards him.

"And what did *you* graduate in?" asked the tiger as he brushed past.

The Party announced a contest for the best sculpture depicting the famous writer Pushkin on his jubilee.

The third prize was awarded for a statue of Pushkin.

The second prize was awarded for a statue of Lenin reading a book by Pushkin.

The first prize was awarded for a statue of Pushkin reading a book by Lenin.

The devil was escorting Brezhnev through hell, and telling him he could choose from a number of punishments.

They came upon Stalin burning in an open flame.

"No, no! Not that!" Brezhnev declared. "What else do you have?"

The devil took him to another area where Hitler was drinking smouldering tar.

"Please! Not that either!" Brezhnev pleaded. "What else do you have?"

The devil then escorted him through a sumptuous chamber where soft lights illuminated a plush sofa upon which Marilyn Monroe was wriggling and squirming, trying to avoid the embrace of Nikita Khrushchev.

"That's it! That's the punishment I want," Brezhnev declared without hesitation. "One just like Nikita's!"

"Sorry," the devil responded. "That's not Nikita's punishment. That's Marilyn Monroe's."

During a Party congress Gorbachev was making glowing promises for the future.

"Comrades, in the future we will have everything if we just stick to our Five Year Plan. Hard work will bring us all kinds of conveniences and luxuries."

He outlined his Five Year Plan: "In the first year there will be housing for everybody. In the second year every apartment will have a private bathroom. In the third year every apartment will have a colour television set. In the fourth year every household will have an automobile. And, finally, in the fifth year, every citizen will have his own aeroplane."

The audience was abuzz with awe and surprise — particularly about the bold assertion of private planes for everyone.

"Comrade President," asked a Politburo member later. "Why will everyone have their own aeroplane?"

"Why, to make life easier, of course," replied Gorbachev. "Just think. What a convenience. For example, a person hears there is food in Vladivostok . . ."

A university professor in Moscow was quizzing his class in a literature seminar.

"Who wrote *Taras Bulba?*" he asked a student.

"I know the answer," the student replied hesitatingly, "but it seems to have slipped my mind."

"All right, then," the professor continued. "Who wrote *Eugene Onegin?*"

"I know that answer," the student said a little more nervously, "but I just can't remember at the moment."

"Well then," the professor declared irritatedly. "Who wrote *War and Peace?*"

"Well, it certainly wasn't me," the student replied in exasperation.

The professor dismissed the class in a huff and left. As he walked down the corridor he mumbled to himself. "Imagine, that student daring to say 'it wasn't me'. Such audacity! Such disrespect for great writers!"

A KGB man mingling with the students overheard him and asked what happened.

"Imagine!" the professor said indignantly. "That student daring to say he didn't write *War and Peace.*"

After many weeks the KGB man met the professor in the hall. "Remember that student who told you he didn't write *War and Peace?*"

"Yes."

"Well, it took us three days, but he finally admitted he wrote it."

A man was running along the streets of Moscow shouting: "The whole country has suffered, because of one man! *One* man has brought us such misery and tears!"

He was immediately seized by the secret police and taken to KGB headquarters for interrogation.

"And just who did you have in mind, comrade, when you shouted that all our problems were due to one man?" the interrogator asked suspiciously.

The man hesitated for a moment, then declared: "Why, Hitler of course."

"Ahhh. Yes. Hitler, indeed," the KGB official said with a smile. "All right, you are free to go."

The man got up to leave, but as he reached the door, he turned and looked at the KGB official: "And who was it that *you* had in mind?"

The chairman of the Council of State of the Democratic Republic of Germany was about to give a rare interview. Seated at his desk, he was almost invisible behind a battery of telephones, giving rise to a question by one journalist about their use.

"These are my links to the countries of our region," began the chairman, obviously proud of his communications set-up. "With this phone I speak to capitalist Germany, with this one to Sweden, with this to Austria, with this to Italy, with this . . ."

"And which phone do you use to speak to Moscow?" broke in the journalist.

"Oh, for that I use these headphones," said the chairman.

In order to answer the persistent question of how far the Soviet people were from true communism, Premier Gorbachev ordered a group of scientists to compute the answer.

They fed all kinds of social, economic, agricultural, and political data into their most sophisticated computer and waited.

Tapes whirred and lights blinked for hours. Finally an answer appeared on the printout: "Twenty-three kilometres."

"What?" the baffled scientists said in unison. "What kind of answer is that? There must be some mistake."

They fed the data in again and out came the same answer: "Twenty-three kilometres."

Finally, a junior technician piped up. "Wait, comrades! It must be correct. After all, remember what our leaders tell us — each Five Year Plan will bring us one more step closer to communism."

A man on a long train ride was bemoaning to himself that he had no-one to talk with.

Soon another man arrived in his compartment and the first man was overjoyed. "I'm so glad you're here," he exclaimed. "I was so bored before you came. Now I can tell you all the new jokes I've heard."

"Before you begin, I want to warn you I'm from the secret police."

"Oh, that's all right," the first man said. "I'll tell the jokes very slowly, and I'll even repeat them for you."

After Brezhnev's death the central committee of the Communist Party met to choose his successor.

After his unanimous election as General Secretary, Yuri Andropov, the former chief of the secret police, announced: "Very well, comrades, now that you have voted, you may lower your arms and come away from the wall."

President Reagan, Prime Minister Thatcher, and Premier Gorbachev are flying to a multinational summit meeting. En route they are discussing whose people are most loyal and obedient.

"The Americans are, of course," President Reagan asserted and offered to demonstrate. He approached an aide and ordered him to jump out of the aeroplane.

"I'm sorry, Mr President, but I can't do it. I have a wife and three children to support."

Mrs Thatcher then tried the same test on one of her British aides.

"I'm sorry, Madame Prime Minister, but I can't do it. I have a wife and three children to support."

Gorbachev then put one of his assistants to the test. "Jump," he ordered to an aide in the Russian entourage. The aide immediately opened the hatch and jumped out.

He landed in the sea where a group of fishermen were hauling their nets and pulled him out of the water, shaken, but alive.

"Why in heavens did you jump out of that aeroplane?" they inquired.

Answered the Russian: "Because I have a wife and three children to support."

In yet another paean to himself, Stalin ordered the printing of a postage stamp bearing his image. He instructed that no expense be spared and that the best materials be used.

Soon, however, complaints filtered back that the new stamps were not sticking to envelopes. Stalin was furious and ordered an immediate investigation.

After a short time the secret police reported back to him. "Tovarish Stalin," a commissar said humbly, "the stamps are in excellent condition. The glue is of the highest quality. The problem is that people are spitting on the wrong side."

Question: What are four reasons for the failure of Soviet agriculture?

Answer: Spring, summer, autumn, and winter.

After the debunking of Stalin in 1956 the Soviets removed him from the mausoleum next to Lenin and encountered a new problem in where to bury him.

They approached the British government to see if he could be buried in England, since Britain was a wartime ally.

"We already have Marx buried here," the British replied. "Two communists of such stature would be too much for us."

The Soviets then approached their colleagues in East Germany.

"We already have Hitler buried here," the Germans replied. "Two such tyrants in one place would be too much for us."

The Israeli government heard of the dilemma and intervened. "Since Stalin fought the Nazis we agree to bury him here," they cabled Moscow.

To which the Kremlin quickly replied: "Thanks, but we'll try elsewhere. Remember you had a resurrection there."

A delegation from the Collective of Soviet Womanhood toured several North African countries. On her return, one of the delegates told her friend about the trip.

"First we arrived in Casablanca. Our breakfast there was luxury itself ... tender crabs' legs in oranges and almonds."

"And then?"

"And then we were brutally raped."

"All of you?" asked her friend, aghast.

"All except Anna. Next, we went to Algiers. That was truly magnificent. We dined on lamb with mint and sesame seeds ... and the wine! It was first-class."

"And then what?"

"We were fiercely raped."

"All of you?"

"All except Anna."

The friend was speechless with incredulity.

"Anyway, we finished the tour in Cairo. Near our hotel was a Turkish bathhouse. There, we anointed ourselves with the oils of all sorts of exotic fruits."

"It sounds wonderful. But what happened then?"

"We were violated without mercy. All except Anna."

"And why not Anna?"

"I don't think she likes Arabs."

After years of research, a multinational group of scientists finally completed a study of the hippopotamus in Africa. Each member then reported their findings.

The German scientist wrote a ten-volume work entitled: "A Short Introduction to the Endocrinology of the Hippopotamus in its Natural Habitat."

The French biologist's paper was called: "How to tell the Sex of a Hippopotamus."

The Russian: "The Dialectical–Materialist Approach to Hippopotamus Biology."

The Bulgarian: "The Bulgarian Hippopotamus as the Loyal Companion of the Heroic Russian Hippopotamus."

The director of the Minsk tractor factory received a call from the local Party committee. In one month his plant was to be inspected by an American trade union delegation. The director called a welder, Smelov, to his office.

"Comrade Smelov," he said, "you know we will shortly be playing host to an American labour delegation. Now, we got rid of all those trouble-making Jews years ago, but you know what these Americans are like; they're sure to ask about the Jewish problem. So, I am asking you, comrade, to assume the identity of a Jewish worker. That way we will have a ready answer for the Yankees."

Smelov, stunned for a few moments, eventually agreed. He received new identity papers and everyone was told to refer to him as Itzak Dimshitz.

When the Americans arrived, they were duly shown around the factory. Sure enough, one of the delegates referred to the Jewish problem.

"Jewish problem?" ejaculated the director, as if personally offended. "What Jewish problem? Many of our most trusted workers are of the Hebrew persuasion. Would you like to meet one? Let me see; yes, there is Comrade Dimshitz, a welder, Party member and one of our best workers."

Turning to a subordinate nearby, the director said, "Ask Comrade Dimshitz to come here."

The subordinate looked nervous. "I'm sorry, Comrade Director, but Dimshitz has already emigrated to Israel."

The well-known nuclear physicist, Dr F. X. Nokitov, hero of the Soviet Union, Order of Lenin, was once asked by a junior colleague to explain Marxist dialectics.

"It's all a matter of science," began the doctor, "but I'll explain it in very simple terms. Imagine that there are two people standing in front of the public baths. One is clean and the other dirty. Who will enter the baths?"

"The dirty one of course," replied the colleague.

"Wrong. You see, the dirty man is like a pig. He is accustomed to living in filth like an animal. He never washes. But a clean man is different. He knows what it is to be washed. Therefore, he will enter the baths. Understand?"

"Yes, certainly," said the junior.

"Take another example. Imagine that there are two people standing in front of the public baths. One is clean and the other is dirty. Who will enter the baths?"

"The clean man, obviously."

"No. Wrong again," said Dr Nokitov, a little indulgently. "The public baths are built for dirty people to make themselves clean. Why should the clean man go in first? He has no need of it. Got it?"

"Well, yes," came the hesitant reply. "I think I understand now."

"Now here's a third example. Imagine, if you will, that there are two people standing in front of the public baths. One is dirty, the other clean. Who will enter the baths?"

The doctor's colleague was totally exasperated by now. "Who the hell knows!"

"Now you've got it!" cried Dr Nokitov. "This is exactly the meaning of Marxist dialectics."

Question: What is meant by the "international solidarity of the proletariat"?

Answer: It is when there is no meat in Moscow and butchers in Budapest are on strike.

An old farmer with his horse-drawn wagon always forded a stream on his way to the village market.

One day he noticed that the Ministry of Roads was constructing a bridge across the stream.

Upon its completion the farmer thought he would try this new convenience and prodded his horse towards the bridge. He stopped at the edge, pondered a moment, then led his horse back to the stream and started crossing it as he always had.

Just as the horse and wagon were in midstream the farmer saw a car drive by and onto the bridge. When it reached the middle, the bridge gave way, sending the car and remnants of the structure into the stream.

"Hmmph!" muttered the farmer disdainfully. "Typical Western tourists. They see a bridge and they cross it."

It is not well known that Russia, like America, regularly sends manned spy planes over its rival's air space. Recently, one plane — the most technologically advanced ever built by the Soviets — was shot down and crashed in a remote part of Alaska. The plane was completely destroyed, but the pilot parachuted to safety. Captured by local troops, he was taken to CIA headquarters in Virginia for interrogation.

"What is your plane called?" began the CIA-bourgeois hoods. "What model is it?"

The pilot, a Soviet patriot to the last, remained silent. Enraged, the American bully-boys began beating him up. Still he did not answer.

"What is the range of your aircraft? Its maximum altitude, speed?" They beat him with rubber hoses, but not a syllable did he utter.

"What kind of radar jamming equipment do you carry? How many onboard computers are there?"

Nothing. They attached electrodes to sensitive parts of his body and gave him electric shocks. Only agonised screams passed this remarkable man's lips.

The Americans were stumped. They vented their frustrations on this brave son of Russia by inflicting every conceivable torture their warped bourgeois minds could invent. Still nothing.

Fortunately for the pilot, the CIA's top man in Romania had been arrested by the KGB. It was arranged that the two men would be swapped.

The pilot, recovering from his ordeal in a Moscow military hospital, was visited by his friends.

"Well, Uri, you look like you had a rough time with those American swine. How was it?"

"Come closer and listen, my comrades," responded Uri in a grave voice. "You've got to study the equipment, know it inside and out. They ask a lot of questions!"

Two Russian military strategists were discussing tactics to use if war occurred.

"If there is war," said one, "we will have agents carry nuclear bombs concealed in suitcases to all the capitals of the Western world — New York, Paris, London, Bonn, Rio de Janeiro..."

"That's an excellent idea, Comrade General," replied his companion. "We certainly have enough bombs for that. But where are we going to get all those suitcases?"

When Chernenko died, he went straight to hell. Upon arrival, Lucifer gave him a choice of three types of punishment.

Lucifer took Chernenko to one area where Lenin was continually being inundated by a massive waterfall. He was perpetually drowning.

"Would you want this punishment?" asked Lucifer.

"No! No!" exclaimed Chernenko. "Show me something else."

Lucifer then took him to another area where Stalin was perpetually burning on a bed of hot coals. His screams told Chernenko that this was not the punishment for him.

Lucifer then guided him to a quiet meadow where birds chirped and flowers bloomed. In the middle of this pastoral scene was a large vat where Khrushchev, Brezhnev and Andropov were standing waist-deep in human excrement.

"This looks quite tolerable," Chernenko reasoned as he joined his comrades in the vat.

Soon after, another devil appeared and announced: "All right. The annual five minute break is over! Everybody back to the handstand!"

The young, intense writer plops himself down at a table in a Moscow cafe. Although a member of the Academy, he thinks of himself as more of a radical, a dissident. As he stirs his thick, strong coffee, he is joined by a friend.

"Hello Alexei," says the friend. "How are you? How are things?"

Immersed in his own world, the writer can only reply: "Bad. I see only gloom."

"Why? Has something happened?"

"Well," says the writer, "they've given me a new apartment in central Moscow. Six rooms and a spa bath."

"Great! You must be really happy."

"No, no. Everything is gloomy."

"So then, there must be other news."

"Yes," admits the troubled young writer. "I did get a summer house on the Black Sea. I only paid 70,000 for it. But that is of passing importance — in the great scheme of things it counts for nothing."

His friend, however, is ecstatic. "But that's wonderful!"

"No. I keep telling you. Everything is bad."

"Something *must* have happened," his friend insists.

"Well, I bought a new car. A Mercedes . . . runs beautifully too."

"Excellent! I'm so glad for you." But the friend can see that this son of the Academy, this heir to Tolstoy and Gorky, is deeply troubled. "Please, Alexei, what is it?"

The writer shakes his bearded head. His frame

begins to shake with uncontrollable sobs. At last, he manages to speak: "Oh, it's just that our people live lives of such ignorance and misery!"